I0005395

Site Name
Description The Site
Website Address   https://
Register Account Name   Register Date
Registration Password   /   /
Password Prompt Questions:

Registration Email
Registration Phone
Instruction Manual

Site Name
Description The Site
Website Address   https://
Register Account Name   Register Date
Registration Password   /   /
Password Prompt Questions:

Registration Email
Registration Phone
Instruction Manual

Site Name
Description The Site
Website Address   https://
Register Account Name   Register Date
Registration Password   /   /
Password Prompt Questions:

Registration Email
Registration Phone
Instruction Manual

Site Name	
Description The Site	

Website Address https://_____

Register Account Name		Register Date
Registration Password		/ /

Password Prompt Questions:

Registration Email	
Registration Phone	
Instruction Manual	

Site Name	
Description The Site	

Website Address https://_____

Register Account Name		Register Date
Registration Password		/ /

Password Prompt Questions:

Registration Email	
Registration Phone	
Instruction Manual	

Site Name	
Description The Site	

Website Address https://_____

Register Account Name		Register Date
Registration Password		/ /

Password Prompt Questions:

Registration Email	
Registration Phone	
Instruction Manual	

Site Name

Description The Site

Website Address   https://

Register Account Name   Register Date

Registration Password   /   /

Password Prompt Questions:

- -

Registration Email

Registration Phone

Instruction Manual

Site Name

Description The Site

Website Address   https://

Register Account Name   Register Date

Registration Password   /   /

Password Prompt Questions:

- -

Registration Email

Registration Phone

Instruction Manual

Site Name

Description The Site

Website Address   https://

Register Account Name   Register Date

Registration Password   /   /

Password Prompt Questions:

- -

Registration Email

Registration Phone

Instruction Manual

Site Name

Description The Site

Website Address   https://_____

Register Account Name   Register Date

Registration Password   /   /

Password Prompt Questions:

Registration Email

Registration Phone

Instruction Manual

Site Name

Description The Site

Website Address   https://_____

Register Account Name   Register Date

Registration Password   /   /

Password Prompt Questions:

Registration Email

Registration Phone

Instruction Manual

Site Name

Description The Site

Website Address   https://_____

Register Account Name   Register Date

Registration Password   /   /

Password Prompt Questions:

Registration Email

Registration Phone

Instruction Manual

Site Name

Description The Site

Website Address https://_____

Register Account Name   Register Date

Registration Password   /   /

Password Prompt Questions:

Registration Email

Registration Phone

Instruction Manual

Site Name

Description The Site

Website Address https://_____

Register Account Name   Register Date

Registration Password   /   /

Password Prompt Questions:

Registration Email

Registration Phone

Instruction Manual

Site Name

Description The Site

Website Address https://_____

Register Account Name   Register Date

Registration Password   /   /

Password Prompt Questions:

Registration Email

Registration Phone

Instruction Manual

Site Name

Description The Site

Website Address https://

Register Account Name		Register Date
Registration Password		/ /

Password Prompt Questions:

Registration Email

Registration Phone

Instruction Manual

Site Name

Description The Site

Website Address https://

Register Account Name		Register Date
Registration Password		/ /

Password Prompt Questions:

Registration Email

Registration Phone

Instruction Manual

Site Name

Description The Site

Website Address https://

Register Account Name		Register Date
Registration Password		/ /

Password Prompt Questions:

Registration Email

Registration Phone

Instruction Manual

Site Name

Description The Site

Website Address https://

Register Account Name   Register Date

Registration Password   /   /

Password Prompt Questions:

Registration Email

Registration Phone

Instruction Manual

Site Name

Description The Site

Website Address https://

Register Account Name   Register Date

Registration Password   /   /

Password Prompt Questions:

Registration Email

Registration Phone

Instruction Manual

Site Name

Description The Site

Website Address https://

Register Account Name   Register Date

Registration Password   /   /

Password Prompt Questions:

Registration Email

Registration Phone

Instruction Manual

Site Name

Description The Site

Website Address   https://

Register Account Name   Register Date

Registration Password   /   /

Password Prompt Questions:

Registration Email

Registration Phone

Instruction Manual

Site Name

Description The Site

Website Address   https://

Register Account Name   Register Date

Registration Password   /   /

Password Prompt Questions:

Registration Email

Registration Phone

Instruction Manual

Site Name

Description The Site

Website Address   https://

Register Account Name   Register Date

Registration Password   /   /

Password Prompt Questions:

Registration Email

Registration Phone

Instruction Manual

Site Name

Description The Site

Website Address   https://

Register Account Name   Register Date

Registration Password   /   /

Password Prompt Questions:

Registration Email

Registration Phone

Instruction Manual

Site Name

Description The Site

Website Address   https://

Register Account Name   Register Date

Registration Password   /   /

Password Prompt Questions:

Registration Email

Registration Phone

Instruction Manual

Site Name

Description The Site

Website Address   https://

Register Account Name   Register Date

Registration Password   /   /

Password Prompt Questions:

Registration Email

Registration Phone

Instruction Manual

Site Name	
Description The Site	
Website Address	https://
Register Account Name	Register Date
Registration Password	/ /
Password Prompt Questions:	
Registration Email	
Registration Phone	
Instruction Manual	

Site Name	
Description The Site	
Website Address	https://
Register Account Name	Register Date
Registration Password	/ /
Password Prompt Questions:	
Registration Email	
Registration Phone	
Instruction Manual	

Site Name	
Description The Site	
Website Address	https://
Register Account Name	Register Date
Registration Password	/ /
Password Prompt Questions:	
Registration Email	
Registration Phone	
Instruction Manual	

Site Name

Description The Site

Website Address   https://_____

Register Account Name   Register Date

Registration Password   /   /

Password Prompt Questions:

Registration Email

Registration Phone

Instruction Manual

Site Name

Description The Site

Website Address   https://_____

Register Account Name   Register Date

Registration Password   /   /

Password Prompt Questions:

Registration Email

Registration Phone

Instruction Manual

Site Name

Description The Site

Website Address   https://_____

Register Account Name   Register Date

Registration Password   /   /

Password Prompt Questions:

Registration Email

Registration Phone

Instruction Manual

Site Name

Description The Site

Website Address   https:// _____

Register Account Name   Register Date

Registration Password   /   /

Password Prompt Questions:

Registration Email

Registration Phone

Instruction Manual

Site Name

Description The Site

Website Address   https:// _____

Register Account Name   Register Date

Registration Password   /   /

Password Prompt Questions:

Registration Email

Registration Phone

Instruction Manual

Site Name

Description The Site

Website Address   https:// _____

Register Account Name   Register Date

Registration Password   /   /

Password Prompt Questions:

Registration Email

Registration Phone

Instruction Manual

Site Name

Description The Site

Website Address   https://_____

Register Account Name   Register Date

Registration Password   /   /

Password Prompt Questions:

Registration Email

Registration Phone

Instruction Manual

Site Name

Description The Site

Website Address   https://_____

Register Account Name   Register Date

Registration Password   /   /

Password Prompt Questions:

Registration Email

Registration Phone

Instruction Manual

Site Name

Description The Site

Website Address   https://_____

Register Account Name   Register Date

Registration Password   /   /

Password Prompt Questions:

Registration Email

Registration Phone

Instruction Manual

Site Name	
Description The Site	
Website Address	https://
Register Account Name	Register Date
Registration Password	/ /
Password Prompt Questions:	
Registration Email	
Registration Phone	
Instruction Manual	

Site Name	
Description The Site	
Website Address	https://
Register Account Name	Register Date
Registration Password	/ /
Password Prompt Questions:	
Registration Email	
Registration Phone	
Instruction Manual	

Site Name	
Description The Site	
Website Address	https://
Register Account Name	Register Date
Registration Password	/ /
Password Prompt Questions:	
Registration Email	
Registration Phone	
Instruction Manual	

Site Name

Description The Site

Website Address   https://

Register Account Name   Register Date

Registration Password   /   /

Password Prompt Questions:

Registration Email

Registration Phone

Instruction Manual

Site Name

Description The Site

Website Address   https://

Register Account Name   Register Date

Registration Password   /   /

Password Prompt Questions:

Registration Email

Registration Phone

Instruction Manual

Site Name

Description The Site

Website Address   https://

Register Account Name   Register Date

Registration Password   /   /

Password Prompt Questions:

Registration Email

Registration Phone

Instruction Manual

Site Name

Description The Site

Website Address   https://_____

Register Account Name   Register Date

Registration Password   /   /

Password Prompt Questions:

Registration Email

Registration Phone

Instruction Manual

Site Name

Description The Site

Website Address   https://_____

Register Account Name   Register Date

Registration Password   /   /

Password Prompt Questions:

Registration Email

Registration Phone

Instruction Manual

Site Name

Description The Site

Website Address   https://_____

Register Account Name   Register Date

Registration Password   /   /

Password Prompt Questions:

Registration Email

Registration Phone

Instruction Manual

Site Name

Description The Site

Website Address https://

Register Account Name   Register Date

Registration Password   /   /

Password Prompt Questions:

Registration Email

Registration Phone

Instruction Manual

Site Name

Description The Site

Website Address https://

Register Account Name   Register Date

Registration Password   /   /

Password Prompt Questions:

Registration Email

Registration Phone

Instruction Manual

Site Name

Description The Site

Website Address https://

Register Account Name   Register Date

Registration Password   /   /

Password Prompt Questions:

Registration Email

Registration Phone

Instruction Manual

Site Name	
Description The Site	
Website Address	https://
Register Account Name	Register Date
Registration Password	/ /
Password Prompt Questions:	
Registration Email	
Registration Phone	
Instruction Manual	

Site Name	
Description The Site	
Website Address	https://
Register Account Name	Register Date
Registration Password	/ /
Password Prompt Questions:	
Registration Email	
Registration Phone	
Instruction Manual	

Site Name	
Description The Site	
Website Address	https://
Register Account Name	Register Date
Registration Password	/ /
Password Prompt Questions:	
Registration Email	
Registration Phone	
Instruction Manual	

Site Name	
Description The Site	
Website Address	https://
Register Account Name	Register Date
Registration Password	/ /
Password Prompt Questions:	

- Registration Email
- Registration Phone
- Instruction Manual

Site Name	
Description The Site	
Website Address	https://
Register Account Name	Register Date
Registration Password	/ /
Password Prompt Questions:	

- Registration Email
- Registration Phone
- Instruction Manual

Site Name	
Description The Site	
Website Address	https://
Register Account Name	Register Date
Registration Password	/ /
Password Prompt Questions:	

- Registration Email
- Registration Phone
- Instruction Manual

Site Name	
Description The Site	
Website Address	https:// _____
Register Account Name	Register Date
Registration Password	/ /
Password Prompt Questions:	
Registration Email	
Registration Phone	
Instruction Manual	

Site Name	
Description The Site	
Website Address	https:// _____
Register Account Name	Register Date
Registration Password	/ /
Password Prompt Questions:	
Registration Email	
Registration Phone	
Instruction Manual	

Site Name	
Description The Site	
Website Address	https:// _____
Register Account Name	Register Date
Registration Password	/ /
Password Prompt Questions:	
Registration Email	
Registration Phone	
Instruction Manual	

Site Name

Description The Site

Website Address   https://

Register Account Name   Register Date

Registration Password   /   /

Password Prompt Questions:

Registration Email

Registration Phone

Instruction Manual

Site Name

Description The Site

Website Address   https://

Register Account Name   Register Date

Registration Password   /   /

Password Prompt Questions:

Registration Email

Registration Phone

Instruction Manual

Site Name

Description The Site

Website Address   https://

Register Account Name   Register Date

Registration Password   /   /

Password Prompt Questions:

Registration Email

Registration Phone

Instruction Manual

Site Name	
Description The Site	
Website Address	https://
Register Account Name	Register Date
Registration Password	/ /
Password Prompt Questions:	

Registration Email	
Registration Phone	
Instruction Manual	

Site Name	
Description The Site	
Website Address	https://
Register Account Name	Register Date
Registration Password	/ /
Password Prompt Questions:	

Registration Email	
Registration Phone	
Instruction Manual	

Site Name	
Description The Site	
Website Address	https://
Register Account Name	Register Date
Registration Password	/ /
Password Prompt Questions:	

Registration Email	
Registration Phone	
Instruction Manual	

Site Name

Description The Site

Website Address   https://_____

Register Account Name   Register Date

Registration Password   /   /

Password Prompt Questions:

- -

Registration Email

Registration Phone

Instruction Manual

Site Name

Description The Site

Website Address   https://_____

Register Account Name   Register Date

Registration Password   /   /

Password Prompt Questions:

- -

Registration Email

Registration Phone

Instruction Manual

Site Name

Description The Site

Website Address   https://_____

Register Account Name   Register Date

Registration Password   /   /

Password Prompt Questions:

- -

Registration Email

Registration Phone

Instruction Manual

Site Name	
Description The Site	
Website Address	https://
Register Account Name	Register Date
Registration Password	/ /
Password Prompt Questions:	
Registration Email	
Registration Phone	
Instruction Manual	

Site Name	
Description The Site	
Website Address	https://
Register Account Name	Register Date
Registration Password	/ /
Password Prompt Questions:	
Registration Email	
Registration Phone	
Instruction Manual	

Site Name	
Description The Site	
Website Address	https://
Register Account Name	Register Date
Registration Password	/ /
Password Prompt Questions:	
Registration Email	
Registration Phone	
Instruction Manual	

Site Name
Description The Site

Website Address   https://_____

Register Account Name   Register Date

Registration Password   /   /

Password Prompt Questions:

Registration Email

Registration Phone

Instruction Manual

Site Name
Description The Site

Website Address   https://_____

Register Account Name   Register Date

Registration Password   /   /

Password Prompt Questions:

Registration Email

Registration Phone

Instruction Manual

Site Name
Description The Site

Website Address   https://_____

Register Account Name   Register Date

Registration Password   /   /

Password Prompt Questions:

Registration Email

Registration Phone

Instruction Manual

Site Name

Description The Site

Website Address   https://_____

Register Account Name   Register Date

Registration Password   /   /

Password Prompt Questions:

Registration Email

Registration Phone

Instruction Manual

Site Name

Description The Site

Website Address   https://_____

Register Account Name   Register Date

Registration Password   /   /

Password Prompt Questions:

Registration Email

Registration Phone

Instruction Manual

Site Name

Description The Site

Website Address   https://_____

Register Account Name   Register Date

Registration Password   /   /

Password Prompt Questions:

Registration Email

Registration Phone

Instruction Manual

Site Name

Description The Site

Website Address https://_____

Register Account Name   Register Date

Registration Password   /   /

Password Prompt Questions:

Registration Email

Registration Phone

Instruction Manual

Site Name

Description The Site

Website Address https://_____

Register Account Name   Register Date

Registration Password   /   /

Password Prompt Questions:

Registration Email

Registration Phone

Instruction Manual

Site Name

Description The Site

Website Address https://_____

Register Account Name   Register Date

Registration Password   /   /

Password Prompt Questions:

Registration Email

Registration Phone

Instruction Manual

Site Name

Description The Site

Website Address   https://

Register Account Name   Register Date

Registration Password   /   /

Password Prompt Questions:

Registration Email

Registration Phone

Instruction Manual

Site Name

Description The Site

Website Address   https://

Register Account Name   Register Date

Registration Password   /   /

Password Prompt Questions:

Registration Email

Registration Phone

Instruction Manual

Site Name

Description The Site

Website Address   https://

Register Account Name   Register Date

Registration Password   /   /

Password Prompt Questions:

Registration Email

Registration Phone

Instruction Manual

Site Name

Description The Site

Website Address   https://_____

Register Account Name   Register Date

Registration Password   /   /

Password Prompt Questions:

- -

Registration Email

Registration Phone

Instruction Manual

Site Name

Description The Site

Website Address   https://_____

Register Account Name   Register Date

Registration Password   /   /

Password Prompt Questions:

- -

Registration Email

Registration Phone

Instruction Manual

Site Name

Description The Site

Website Address   https://_____

Register Account Name   Register Date

Registration Password   /   /

Password Prompt Questions:

- -

Registration Email

Registration Phone

Instruction Manual

Site Name	
Description The Site	
Website Address	https://
Register Account Name	Register Date
Registration Password	/ /
Password Prompt Questions:	
Registration Email	
Registration Phone	
Instruction Manual	

Site Name	
Description The Site	
Website Address	https://
Register Account Name	Register Date
Registration Password	/ /
Password Prompt Questions:	
Registration Email	
Registration Phone	
Instruction Manual	

Site Name	
Description The Site	
Website Address	https://
Register Account Name	Register Date
Registration Password	/ /
Password Prompt Questions:	
Registration Email	
Registration Phone	
Instruction Manual	

Site Name

Description The Site

Website Address   https://_____

Register Account Name   Register Date

Registration Password   /   /

Password Prompt Questions:

- -

Registration Email

Registration Phone

Instruction Manual

Site Name

Description The Site

Website Address   https://_____

Register Account Name   Register Date

Registration Password   /   /

Password Prompt Questions:

- -

Registration Email

Registration Phone

Instruction Manual

Site Name

Description The Site

Website Address   https://_____

Register Account Name   Register Date

Registration Password   /   /

Password Prompt Questions:

- -

Registration Email

Registration Phone

Instruction Manual

Site Name

Description The Site

Website Address   https://

Register Account Name   Register Date

Registration Password   /   /

Password Prompt Questions:

Registration Email

Registration Phone

Instruction Manual

Site Name

Description The Site

Website Address   https://

Register Account Name   Register Date

Registration Password   /   /

Password Prompt Questions:

Registration Email

Registration Phone

Instruction Manual

Site Name

Description The Site

Website Address   https://

Register Account Name   Register Date

Registration Password   /   /

Password Prompt Questions:

Registration Email

Registration Phone

Instruction Manual

Site Name

Description The Site

Website Address   https://

Register Account Name   Register Date

Registration Password   /   /

Password Prompt Questions:

Registration Email

Registration Phone

Instruction Manual

Site Name

Description The Site

Website Address   https://

Register Account Name   Register Date

Registration Password   /   /

Password Prompt Questions:

Registration Email

Registration Phone

Instruction Manual

Site Name

Description The Site

Website Address   https://

Register Account Name   Register Date

Registration Password   /   /

Password Prompt Questions:

Registration Email

Registration Phone

Instruction Manual

Site Name	
Description The Site	
Website Address	https://
Register Account Name	Register Date
Registration Password	/ /
Password Prompt Questions:	
Registration Email	
Registration Phone	
Instruction Manual	

Site Name	
Description The Site	
Website Address	https://
Register Account Name	Register Date
Registration Password	/ /
Password Prompt Questions:	
Registration Email	
Registration Phone	
Instruction Manual	

Site Name	
Description The Site	
Website Address	https://
Register Account Name	Register Date
Registration Password	/ /
Password Prompt Questions:	
Registration Email	
Registration Phone	
Instruction Manual	

Site Name

Description The Site

Website Address   https://_____

Register Account Name   Register Date

Registration Password   /   /

Password Prompt Questions:

Registration Email

Registration Phone

Instruction Manual

Site Name

Description The Site

Website Address   https://_____

Register Account Name   Register Date

Registration Password   /   /

Password Prompt Questions:

Registration Email

Registration Phone

Instruction Manual

Site Name

Description The Site

Website Address   https://_____

Register Account Name   Register Date

Registration Password   /   /

Password Prompt Questions:

Registration Email

Registration Phone

Instruction Manual

Site Name
Description The Site

Website Address https://_____

Register Account Name   Register Date

Registration Password   / _____ / _____

Password Prompt Questions:
- -

Registration Email

Registration Phone

Instruction Manual

Site Name
Description The Site

Website Address https://_____

Register Account Name   Register Date

Registration Password   / _____ / _____

Password Prompt Questions:
- -

Registration Email

Registration Phone

Instruction Manual

Site Name
Description The Site

Website Address https://_____

Register Account Name   Register Date

Registration Password   / _____ / _____

Password Prompt Questions:
- -

Registration Email

Registration Phone

Instruction Manual

Site Name

Description The Site

Website Address   https://_____

Register Account Name   Register Date

Registration Password   /   /

Password Prompt Questions:

Registration Email

Registration Phone

Instruction Manual

Site Name

Description The Site

Website Address   https://_____

Register Account Name   Register Date

Registration Password   /   /

Password Prompt Questions:

Registration Email

Registration Phone

Instruction Manual

Site Name

Description The Site

Website Address   https://_____

Register Account Name   Register Date

Registration Password   /   /

Password Prompt Questions:

Registration Email

Registration Phone

Instruction Manual

Site Name

Description The Site

Website Address https://_____

Register Account Name   Register Date

Registration Password   /   /

Password Prompt Questions:

Registration Email

Registration Phone

Instruction Manual

Site Name

Description The Site

Website Address https://_____

Register Account Name   Register Date

Registration Password   /   /

Password Prompt Questions:

Registration Email

Registration Phone

Instruction Manual

Site Name

Description The Site

Website Address https://_____

Register Account Name   Register Date

Registration Password   /   /

Password Prompt Questions:

Registration Email

Registration Phone

Instruction Manual

Site Name

Description The Site

Website Address https://

Register Account Name   Register Date

Registration Password   /   /

Password Prompt Questions:

Registration Email

Registration Phone

Instruction Manual

Site Name

Description The Site

Website Address https://

Register Account Name   Register Date

Registration Password   /   /

Password Prompt Questions:

Registration Email

Registration Phone

Instruction Manual

Site Name

Description The Site

Website Address https://

Register Account Name   Register Date

Registration Password   /   /

Password Prompt Questions:

Registration Email

Registration Phone

Instruction Manual

Site Name
Description The Site

Website Address https://_____

Register Account Name		Register Date
Registration Password		/ /

Password Prompt Questions:

Registration Email

Registration Phone

Instruction Manual

Site Name
Description The Site

Website Address https://_____

Register Account Name		Register Date
Registration Password		/ /

Password Prompt Questions:

Registration Email

Registration Phone

Instruction Manual

Site Name
Description The Site

Website Address https://_____

Register Account Name		Register Date
Registration Password		/ /

Password Prompt Questions:

Registration Email

Registration Phone

Instruction Manual

Site Name	
Description The Site	
Website Address	https://
Register Account Name	Register Date
Registration Password	/ /
Password Prompt Questions:	

Registration Email	
Registration Phone	
Instruction Manual	

Site Name	
Description The Site	
Website Address	https://
Register Account Name	Register Date
Registration Password	/ /
Password Prompt Questions:	

Registration Email	
Registration Phone	
Instruction Manual	

Site Name	
Description The Site	
Website Address	https://
Register Account Name	Register Date
Registration Password	/ /
Password Prompt Questions:	

Registration Email	
Registration Phone	
Instruction Manual	

Site Name	
Description The Site	
Website Address	https:// _____
Register Account Name	Register Date
Registration Password	/ /
Password Prompt Questions:	
--	
Registration Email	
Registration Phone	
Instruction Manual	

Site Name	
Description The Site	
Website Address	https:// _____
Register Account Name	Register Date
Registration Password	/ /
Password Prompt Questions:	
--	
Registration Email	
Registration Phone	
Instruction Manual	

Site Name	
Description The Site	
Website Address	https:// _____
Register Account Name	Register Date
Registration Password	/ /
Password Prompt Questions:	
--	
Registration Email	
Registration Phone	
Instruction Manual	

Site Name

Description The Site

Website Address   https://_____

Register Account Name   Register Date

Registration Password   /   /

Password Prompt Questions:

Registration Email

Registration Phone

Instruction Manual

Site Name

Description The Site

Website Address   https://_____

Register Account Name   Register Date

Registration Password   /   /

Password Prompt Questions:

Registration Email

Registration Phone

Instruction Manual

Site Name

Description The Site

Website Address   https://_____

Register Account Name   Register Date

Registration Password   /   /

Password Prompt Questions:

Registration Email

Registration Phone

Instruction Manual

Site Name

Description The Site

Website Address   https://_____

Register Account Name   Register Date

Registration Password   /   /

Password Prompt Questions:

Registration Email

Registration Phone

Instruction Manual

Site Name

Description The Site

Website Address   https://_____

Register Account Name   Register Date

Registration Password   /   /

Password Prompt Questions:

Registration Email

Registration Phone

Instruction Manual

Site Name

Description The Site

Website Address   https://_____

Register Account Name   Register Date

Registration Password   /   /

Password Prompt Questions:

Registration Email

Registration Phone

Instruction Manual

Site Name

Description The Site

Website Address   https://_____

Register Account Name   Register Date

Registration Password   /   /

Password Prompt Questions:

- -

Registration Email

Registration Phone

Instruction Manual

Site Name

Description The Site

Website Address   https://_____

Register Account Name   Register Date

Registration Password   /   /

Password Prompt Questions:

- -

Registration Email

Registration Phone

Instruction Manual

Site Name

Description The Site

Website Address   https://_____

Register Account Name   Register Date

Registration Password   /   /

Password Prompt Questions:

- -

Registration Email

Registration Phone

Instruction Manual

Site Name	
Description The Site	
Website Address	https://
Register Account Name	Register Date
Registration Password	/ /
Password Prompt Questions:	
Registration Email	
Registration Phone	
Instruction Manual	

Site Name	
Description The Site	
Website Address	https://
Register Account Name	Register Date
Registration Password	/ /
Password Prompt Questions:	
Registration Email	
Registration Phone	
Instruction Manual	

Site Name	
Description The Site	
Website Address	https://
Register Account Name	Register Date
Registration Password	/ /
Password Prompt Questions:	
Registration Email	
Registration Phone	
Instruction Manual	

Site Name
Description The Site

Website Address   https://_____

Register Account Name   Register Date

Registration Password   /   /

Password Prompt Questions:

Registration Email

Registration Phone

Instruction Manual

Site Name
Description The Site

Website Address   https://_____

Register Account Name   Register Date

Registration Password   /   /

Password Prompt Questions:

Registration Email

Registration Phone

Instruction Manual

Site Name
Description The Site

Website Address   https://_____

Register Account Name   Register Date

Registration Password   /   /

Password Prompt Questions:

Registration Email

Registration Phone

Instruction Manual

Site Name

Description The Site

Website Address   https://_____

Register Account Name   Register Date

Registration Password   /   /

Password Prompt Questions:

Registration Email

Registration Phone

Instruction Manual

Site Name

Description The Site

Website Address   https://_____

Register Account Name   Register Date

Registration Password   /   /

Password Prompt Questions:

Registration Email

Registration Phone

Instruction Manual

Site Name

Description The Site

Website Address   https://_____

Register Account Name   Register Date

Registration Password   /   /

Password Prompt Questions:

Registration Email

Registration Phone

Instruction Manual

Site Name

Description The Site

Website Address   https://_____

Register Account Name   Register Date

Registration Password   /   /

Password Prompt Questions:

Registration Email

Registration Phone

Instruction Manual

Site Name

Description The Site

Website Address   https://_____

Register Account Name   Register Date

Registration Password   /   /

Password Prompt Questions:

Registration Email

Registration Phone

Instruction Manual

Site Name

Description The Site

Website Address   https://_____

Register Account Name   Register Date

Registration Password   /   /

Password Prompt Questions:

Registration Email

Registration Phone

Instruction Manual

Site Name	
Description The Site	
Website Address	https://
Register Account Name	Register Date
Registration Password	/ /
Password Prompt Questions:	

Registration Email	
Registration Phone	
Instruction Manual	

Site Name	
Description The Site	
Website Address	https://
Register Account Name	Register Date
Registration Password	/ /
Password Prompt Questions:	

Registration Email	
Registration Phone	
Instruction Manual	

Site Name	
Description The Site	
Website Address	https://
Register Account Name	Register Date
Registration Password	/ /
Password Prompt Questions:	

Registration Email	
Registration Phone	
Instruction Manual	

Site Name

Description The Site

Website Address https://_____

Register Account Name   Register Date

Registration Password   /   /

Password Prompt Questions:

Registration Email

Registration Phone

Instruction Manual

Site Name

Description The Site

Website Address https://_____

Register Account Name   Register Date

Registration Password   /   /

Password Prompt Questions:

Registration Email

Registration Phone

Instruction Manual

Site Name

Description The Site

Website Address https://_____

Register Account Name   Register Date

Registration Password   /   /

Password Prompt Questions:

Registration Email

Registration Phone

Instruction Manual

Site Name	
Description The Site	
Website Address	https://
Register Account Name	Register Date
Registration Password	/ /
Password Prompt Questions:	
Registration Email	
Registration Phone	
Instruction Manual	

Site Name	
Description The Site	
Website Address	https://
Register Account Name	Register Date
Registration Password	/ /
Password Prompt Questions:	
Registration Email	
Registration Phone	
Instruction Manual	

Site Name	
Description The Site	
Website Address	https://
Register Account Name	Register Date
Registration Password	/ /
Password Prompt Questions:	
Registration Email	
Registration Phone	
Instruction Manual	

Site Name	
Description The Site	
Website Address	https://
Register Account Name	Register Date
Registration Password	/ /
Password Prompt Questions:	
Registration Email	
Registration Phone	
Instruction Manual	

Site Name	
Description The Site	
Website Address	https://
Register Account Name	Register Date
Registration Password	/ /
Password Prompt Questions:	
Registration Email	
Registration Phone	
Instruction Manual	

Site Name	
Description The Site	
Website Address	https://
Register Account Name	Register Date
Registration Password	/ /
Password Prompt Questions:	
Registration Email	
Registration Phone	
Instruction Manual	

Site Name

Description The Site

Website Address   https://

Register Account Name   Register Date

Registration Password   /   /

Password Prompt Questions:

Registration Email

Registration Phone

Instruction Manual

Site Name

Description The Site

Website Address   https://

Register Account Name   Register Date

Registration Password   /   /

Password Prompt Questions:

Registration Email

Registration Phone

Instruction Manual

Site Name

Description The Site

Website Address   https://

Register Account Name   Register Date

Registration Password   /   /

Password Prompt Questions:

Registration Email

Registration Phone

Instruction Manual

Site Name

Description The Site

Website Address   https://_____

Register Account Name   Register Date

Registration Password   /   /

Password Prompt Questions:
- -

Registration Email

Registration Phone

Instruction Manual

Site Name

Description The Site

Website Address   https://_____

Register Account Name   Register Date

Registration Password   /   /

Password Prompt Questions:
- -

Registration Email

Registration Phone

Instruction Manual

Site Name

Description The Site

Website Address   https://_____

Register Account Name   Register Date

Registration Password   /   /

Password Prompt Questions:
- -

Registration Email

Registration Phone

Instruction Manual

Site Name

Description The Site

Website Address   https://

Register Account Name   Register Date

Registration Password   /   /

Password Prompt Questions:

Registration Email

Registration Phone

Instruction Manual

Site Name

Description The Site

Website Address   https://

Register Account Name   Register Date

Registration Password   /   /

Password Prompt Questions:

Registration Email

Registration Phone

Instruction Manual

Site Name

Description The Site

Website Address   https://

Register Account Name   Register Date

Registration Password   /   /

Password Prompt Questions:

Registration Email

Registration Phone

Instruction Manual

Site Name

Description The Site

Website Address   https:// _____

Register Account Name   Register Date

Registration Password   /   /

Password Prompt Questions:

Registration Email

Registration Phone

Instruction Manual

Site Name

Description The Site

Website Address   https:// _____

Register Account Name   Register Date

Registration Password   /   /

Password Prompt Questions:

Registration Email

Registration Phone

Instruction Manual

Site Name

Description The Site

Website Address   https:// _____

Register Account Name   Register Date

Registration Password   /   /

Password Prompt Questions:

Registration Email

Registration Phone

Instruction Manual

Site Name

Description The Site

Website Address   https://

Register Account Name   Register Date

Registration Password   /   /

Password Prompt Questions:

Registration Email

Registration Phone

Instruction Manual

Site Name

Description The Site

Website Address   https://

Register Account Name   Register Date

Registration Password   /   /

Password Prompt Questions:

Registration Email

Registration Phone

Instruction Manual

Site Name

Description The Site

Website Address   https://

Register Account Name   Register Date

Registration Password   /   /

Password Prompt Questions:

Registration Email

Registration Phone

Instruction Manual

Site Name

Description The Site

Website Address https://

Register Account Name   Register Date

Registration Password   /   /

Password Prompt Questions:

Registration Email

Registration Phone

Instruction Manual

Site Name

Description The Site

Website Address https://

Register Account Name   Register Date

Registration Password   /   /

Password Prompt Questions:

Registration Email

Registration Phone

Instruction Manual

Site Name

Description The Site

Website Address https://

Register Account Name   Register Date

Registration Password   /   /

Password Prompt Questions:

Registration Email

Registration Phone

Instruction Manual

Site Name

Description The Site

Website Address   https://

Register Account Name   Register Date

Registration Password   /   /

Password Prompt Questions:

Registration Email

Registration Phone

Instruction Manual

Site Name

Description The Site

Website Address   https://

Register Account Name   Register Date

Registration Password   /   /

Password Prompt Questions:

Registration Email

Registration Phone

Instruction Manual

Site Name

Description The Site

Website Address   https://

Register Account Name   Register Date

Registration Password   /   /

Password Prompt Questions:

Registration Email

Registration Phone

Instruction Manual

Site Name

Description The Site

Website Address   https://_____

Register Account Name   Register Date

Registration Password   /   /

Password Prompt Questions:

Registration Email

Registration Phone

Instruction Manual

Site Name

Description The Site

Website Address   https://_____

Register Account Name   Register Date

Registration Password   /   /

Password Prompt Questions:

Registration Email

Registration Phone

Instruction Manual

Site Name

Description The Site

Website Address   https://_____

Register Account Name   Register Date

Registration Password   /   /

Password Prompt Questions:

Registration Email

Registration Phone

Instruction Manual

Site Name

Description The Site

Website Address   https://_____

Register Account Name   Register Date

Registration Password   /   /

Password Prompt Questions:

Registration Email

Registration Phone

Instruction Manual

Site Name

Description The Site

Website Address   https://_____

Register Account Name   Register Date

Registration Password   /   /

Password Prompt Questions:

Registration Email

Registration Phone

Instruction Manual

Site Name

Description The Site

Website Address   https://_____

Register Account Name   Register Date

Registration Password   /   /

Password Prompt Questions:

Registration Email

Registration Phone

Instruction Manual

Site Name

Description The Site

Website Address https://

Register Account Name   Register Date

Registration Password   /   /

Password Prompt Questions:

Registration Email

Registration Phone

Instruction Manual

Site Name

Description The Site

Website Address https://

Register Account Name   Register Date

Registration Password   /   /

Password Prompt Questions:

Registration Email

Registration Phone

Instruction Manual

Site Name

Description The Site

Website Address https://

Register Account Name   Register Date

Registration Password   /   /

Password Prompt Questions:

Registration Email

Registration Phone

Instruction Manual

Site Name

Description The Site

Website Address   https://

Register Account Name   Register Date

Registration Password   /   /

Password Prompt Questions:

Registration Email

Registration Phone

Instruction Manual

Site Name

Description The Site

Website Address   https://

Register Account Name   Register Date

Registration Password   /   /

Password Prompt Questions:

Registration Email

Registration Phone

Instruction Manual

Site Name

Description The Site

Website Address   https://

Register Account Name   Register Date

Registration Password   /   /

Password Prompt Questions:

Registration Email

Registration Phone

Instruction Manual

Site Name

Description The Site

Website Address https://

Register Account Name   Register Date

Registration Password   /   /

Password Prompt Questions:

Registration Email

Registration Phone

Instruction Manual

Site Name

Description The Site

Website Address https://

Register Account Name   Register Date

Registration Password   /   /

Password Prompt Questions:

Registration Email

Registration Phone

Instruction Manual

Site Name

Description The Site

Website Address https://

Register Account Name   Register Date

Registration Password   /   /

Password Prompt Questions:

Registration Email

Registration Phone

Instruction Manual

Site Name

Description The Site

Website Address   https://

Register Account Name   Register Date

Registration Password   /   /

Password Prompt Questions:

Registration Email

Registration Phone

Instruction Manual

Site Name

Description The Site

Website Address   https://

Register Account Name   Register Date

Registration Password   /   /

Password Prompt Questions:

Registration Email

Registration Phone

Instruction Manual

Site Name

Description The Site

Website Address   https://

Register Account Name   Register Date

Registration Password   /   /

Password Prompt Questions:

Registration Email

Registration Phone

Instruction Manual

Site Name

Description The Site

Website Address   https://

Register Account Name   Register Date

Registration Password   /   /

Password Prompt Questions:

Registration Email

Registration Phone

Instruction Manual

Site Name

Description The Site

Website Address   https://

Register Account Name   Register Date

Registration Password   /   /

Password Prompt Questions:

Registration Email

Registration Phone

Instruction Manual

Site Name

Description The Site

Website Address   https://

Register Account Name   Register Date

Registration Password   /   /

Password Prompt Questions:

Registration Email

Registration Phone

Instruction Manual

Site Name

Description The Site

Website Address   https://_____

Register Account Name   Register Date

Registration Password   /   /

Password Prompt Questions:

- -

Registration Email

Registration Phone

Instruction Manual

Site Name

Description The Site

Website Address   https://_____

Register Account Name   Register Date

Registration Password   /   /

Password Prompt Questions:

- -

Registration Email

Registration Phone

Instruction Manual

Site Name

Description The Site

Website Address   https://_____

Register Account Name   Register Date

Registration Password   /   /

Password Prompt Questions:

- -

Registration Email

Registration Phone

Instruction Manual

Site Name

Description The Site

Website Address   https://

Register Account Name   Register Date

Registration Password   /   /

Password Prompt Questions:

- -

Registration Email

Registration Phone

Instruction Manual

Site Name

Description The Site

Website Address   https://

Register Account Name   Register Date

Registration Password   /   /

Password Prompt Questions:

- -

Registration Email

Registration Phone

Instruction Manual

Site Name

Description The Site

Website Address   https://

Register Account Name   Register Date

Registration Password   /   /

Password Prompt Questions:

- -

Registration Email

Registration Phone

Instruction Manual

Site Name

Description The Site

Website Address   https://

Register Account Name   Register Date

Registration Password   /   /

Password Prompt Questions:

Registration Email

Registration Phone

Instruction Manual

Site Name

Description The Site

Website Address   https://

Register Account Name   Register Date

Registration Password   /   /

Password Prompt Questions:

Registration Email

Registration Phone

Instruction Manual

Site Name

Description The Site

Website Address   https://

Register Account Name   Register Date

Registration Password   /   /

Password Prompt Questions:

Registration Email

Registration Phone

Instruction Manual

Site Name

Description The Site

Website Address   https://

Register Account Name   Register Date

Registration Password   /   /

Password Prompt Questions:

- -

Registration Email

Registration Phone

Instruction Manual

Site Name

Description The Site

Website Address   https://

Register Account Name   Register Date

Registration Password   /   /

Password Prompt Questions:

- -

Registration Email

Registration Phone

Instruction Manual

Site Name

Description The Site

Website Address   https://

Register Account Name   Register Date

Registration Password   /   /

Password Prompt Questions:

- -

Registration Email

Registration Phone

Instruction Manual

Site Name	
Description The Site	
Website Address	https://
Register Account Name	Register Date
Registration Password	/ /
Password Prompt Questions:	
Registration Email	
Registration Phone	
Instruction Manual	

Site Name	
Description The Site	
Website Address	https://
Register Account Name	Register Date
Registration Password	/ /
Password Prompt Questions:	
Registration Email	
Registration Phone	
Instruction Manual	

Site Name	
Description The Site	
Website Address	https://
Register Account Name	Register Date
Registration Password	/ /
Password Prompt Questions:	
Registration Email	
Registration Phone	
Instruction Manual	

Site Name	
Description The Site	
Website Address	https://
Register Account Name	Register Date
Registration Password	/ /
Password Prompt Questions:	

Registration Email	
Registration Phone	
Instruction Manual	

Site Name	
Description The Site	
Website Address	https://
Register Account Name	Register Date
Registration Password	/ /
Password Prompt Questions:	

Registration Email	
Registration Phone	
Instruction Manual	

Site Name	
Description The Site	
Website Address	https://
Register Account Name	Register Date
Registration Password	/ /
Password Prompt Questions:	

Registration Email	
Registration Phone	
Instruction Manual	

Site Name	
Description The Site	
Website Address	https://
Register Account Name	Register Date
Registration Password	/ /

Password Prompt Questions:

Registration Email	
Registration Phone	
Instruction Manual	

Site Name	
Description The Site	
Website Address	https://
Register Account Name	Register Date
Registration Password	/ /

Password Prompt Questions:

Registration Email	
Registration Phone	
Instruction Manual	

Site Name	
Description The Site	
Website Address	https://
Register Account Name	Register Date
Registration Password	/ /

Password Prompt Questions:

Registration Email	
Registration Phone	
Instruction Manual	

Site Name

Description The Site

Website Address https://_____

Register Account Name   Register Date

Registration Password   /   /

Password Prompt Questions:

- -

Registration Email

Registration Phone

Instruction Manual

Site Name

Description The Site

Website Address https://_____

Register Account Name   Register Date

Registration Password   /   /

Password Prompt Questions:

- -

Registration Email

Registration Phone

Instruction Manual

Site Name

Description The Site

Website Address https://_____

Register Account Name   Register Date

Registration Password   /   /

Password Prompt Questions:

- -

Registration Email

Registration Phone

Instruction Manual

www.ingramcontent.com/pod-product-compliance
Lightning Source LLC
Chambersburg PA
CBHW071029050326
40689CB00014B/3584